THE OFFICIAL  SPORT
FORMULAONE
ANNUAL 2012

Written by David Clayton
Designed by Simon Thorley

itv STUDIOS

The ITV Sport logo is licensed
by ITV Studios Global Entertainment.
All rights reserved.

A Grange Publication

© 2011. Published by Grange Communications Ltd., Edinburgh,
under licence from ITV Studios Global Entertainment. Printed in
the EU.

Photographs © Action Images

Dedication: For Jordan & Melissa Cain

ISBN 978 1 908221 25 4

£7.99

CONTENTS

2010FORMULAONE
SEASONREVIEW

AN OVERVIEW OF ONE OF THE MOST EXCITING FORMULA ONE SEASONS IN MANY YEARS…

Sebastian Vettel became the youngest World Champion in Formula One history when he completed an exciting season by winning the Abu Dhabi Grand Prix on the final day.

It was Formula One's 61st season in total and it also proved to be one of the best with the battle to be champion going right to the wire and it was fitting that the dramatic nature of the sport should go into the last day with four drivers all having the chance of winning the coveted title of Formula One champion. But that was all a distant dream when the season began in Bahrain on March 14, 2010. With 19 races in 18 different countries, the battle was about to begin and the racing world held its breath as each team unveiled its latest car and more importantly, newest engine.

After months of tests and pre-season racing, the Bahrain Grand Prix finally began and it was Ferrari's latest acquisition, Fernando Alonso, who climbed the podium as winner, though the victory celebrations were evenly spread in the first few races with reigning champion Jenson Button triumphing in Australia and Vettel claiming his first win of the season in Malaysia. Already the World Championship leader had entered each race and failed to win – a trend that would continue throughout the season so that topping the leader board meant failure to win the next race!

Button clocked up his second victory of the season in China in race four, but Australia's Mark Webber followed that with successive victories in Spain and Monaco – it was the most open title race in living memory and the race fans were lapping it up all over the world.

Webber looked to be on his way to a hat-trick of victories at the Turkish Grand Prix when he was involved in a collision with Red Bull team-mate Vettel which saw the latter retire from the race and Webber finish third allowing Lewis Hamilton to claim his first win of the season, a feat he repeated by winning the Canadian Grand Prix next time out.

Britain's other golden boy Jenson Button was still in touch with the leaders, though it was

clear he was not about dominate in the way he had done in 2009. Controversy raged in the European Grand Prix in Valencia with Webber crashing and Hamilton incurring a drive-through penalty for passing the Safety Car shortly after the accident. Vettel went on to win with Hamilton still claiming second and more vital points.

Red Bull dominated the headlines at the British Grand Prix when a decision to take part of Mark Webber's car and repair team-mate Sebastian Vettel's clarified who the owner believed was the more important of his two drivers – but when Vettel suffered an early puncture, it was Webber who went on to win his third race of the season and perhaps prove a point, too.

Ferrari bounced back in style at the German Grand Prix with Alonso and Felipe Massa finishing first and second, though it appeared the then-leader Massa was instructed to move over and let his team-mate pass at one point. This led to numerous accusations and an enquiry that Ferrari were eventually cleared of – it is against the rules of Formula One to let a team-mate pass!

Mark Webber's chances of becoming champion increased with a fourth 2010 Formula One victory in Hungary, this after Vettel had been demoted to third for a Safety Car infringement. Lewis Hamilton was not about to give up hopes of a second World Championship and a skilful drive at a wet Belgian Grand Prix saw him record his third win of the season – it seemed as though every race could be won by any one of ten drivers and it added even more excitement to the sport for the fans who followed the races in their millions.

The European part of the season ended with Fernando Alonso claiming victory in Italy and he won his fourth race of 2010 with victory in Singapore – suddenly the 2006 World Champion looked as though he may add a third championship to his already impressive CV.

It was in Japan, however, that Red Bull really began to dominate with Vettel first and Webber

2010 FORMULA ONE
SEASON REVIEW

second, though Alonso kept his points tally ticking along nicely with a third-place finish and things got even better for the Spaniard in Korea when both Red Bull drivers failed to finish and Alonso claimed win number five of a season that just kept getting better for him.

But Red Bull resumed normal service in Brazil when Vettel and Webber again made it a one-two finish and also claimed the World Constructors' Championship for their team – all that was needed now to cap a perfect year was for one of their talented drivers to take their maiden World Champion title.

FINAL STANDINGS (TOP 10):

1. Sebastian Vettel (Ger) Red Bull 256 points
2. Fernando Alonso (Spa) Ferrari 252 points
3. Mark Webber (Aus) Red Bull 242 points
4. Lewis Hamilton (GB) McLaren 240 points
5. Jenson Button (GB) McLaren 214 points
6. Felipe Massa (Bra) Ferrari 144 points
7. Nico Rosberg (Ger) Mercedes 142 points
8. Robert Kubica (Pol) Renault 136 points
9. Michael Schumacher (Ger) Mercedes 72 points
10. Rubens Barrichello (Bra) Williams 47 points

It all came down to one race – the Abu Dhabi Grand Prix – the final battle of an epic season. While both Vettel and Webber could win, so could Alonso who needed only to finish fourth. Lewis Hamilton needed several scenarios to happen for him to win the title, but that wouldn't stop him giving his all to see where it took him.

In an epic battle that swayed one way, then the other, Germany's Sebastian Vettel eventually won with Lewis Hamilton and Jenson Button coming in second and third respectively. Vettel had topped the World Championship for the first time – and it just happened to be the one that mattered most – on the final day!

WORLDCHAMPION
SebastianVettel

20 THINGS YOU NEED TO KNOW...

1) He was born on July 3, 1987 in Heppenheim, Germany.

2) His childhood heroes are "The three Michaels", who were Michael Schumacher, Michael Jackson and Michael Jordan.

3) His first love is not only motorsport – he is a huge fan of German football side Eintracht Frankfurt.

4) He began his karting career at the age of seven in 1995 and used to race around his garden repeatedly! He soon entered junior races and began to collect his first trophies.

5) In 2001, aged 14, he won several karting titles as his star began to rise, including European Junior Kart Championship, German Junior Kart Championship, Monaco Junior Kart Cup and Kart Paris-Bercy.

6) After progressing to open-wheel racing in 2003, Vettel finished runner-up in the Formula BMW ADAC Championship and was the highest-placed rookie.

7) A year later he dominated the Formula BMW ADAC Championship with 18 wins from 20 races, including 15 pole positions and 16 fastest laps as he bacome one of the world's most promising talents – he was still just 17 years old at this point!

8) Nothing, it seems, could stop Vettel's rise to the top and in 2005 he moved into the Formula 3 Euro Series and again was the best rookie, taking six podiums on his way to finishing fifth overall.

9) After finishing second in Formula 3 Euro Series 12 months later with three wins, Vettel was named as test driver with BMW Sauber, becoming the youngest to drive at a Grand Prix event when he took part in a practice session prior to the Istanbul race aged **19 years and 53 days**.

10) In 2007 Vettel finally got his big chance and took it in style after replacing Robert Kubica for USA GP following Kubica's crash in the previous race in Canada. He finished eighth, thus becoming the youngest driver ever to score a point.

11) Toro Rosso quickly saw Vettel's promise and he replaced Scott Speed and quickly repaid their faith, despite crashing at the Japanese Grand Prix where he was poised for a top-three finish. The talented German scored the team's first points a week later in China after finishing fourth.

12) In 2008, Vettel became the youngest to qualify on pole and youngest race winner at the Italian Grand Prix while driving for Toro Rosso and finished his first full season eighth in the standings with 35 points.

13) Vettel replaced David Coulthard at Red Bull Racing for the 2009 season and named his first Red Bull car of 2009 'Kate' saying: "Like a ship, it should be named after a girl as it's sexy."

14) On his debut in Australia he collected a 10-place grid penalty for the next race in Malaysia for attempting to finish with three wheels!

15) Two races later in the season he secured Red Bull's first pole position and victory in the third Grand Prix of the year in China. He went on to win three more races in Britain, Japan and Abu Dhabi and finished runner-up in the championship – it seemed just a matter of time before he was crowned world champ...

16) Vettel was unstoppable as he won the Malaysian, European (Valencia), Japanese, Brazilian and Abu Dhabi Grand Prix on his way to becoming the youngest champion in Formula One history at 23 years 135 days. He topped the leader board for the first time

after the final race of the 2010 season – an incredible achievement and no doubt the first of many. His tally of 256 was also a new Formula One record.

17) For the past four years Vettel has teamed up with his boyhood idol Michael Schumacher to win the Nation's Cup at the Race of Champions – the annual event where drivers from all the leading motorsports on the planet gather to find out who is the Champion of Champions.

18) Vettel began the 2011 Formula One season in style, winning five of the first six races to open a sizeable gap at the top of the Drivers World Championship as he looked to retain his title.

19) Though Schumacher remains his hero, Vettel has claimed he doesn't want to be known as 'Baby Schumi' – just the 'New Vettel'.

20) Despite holding nine Formula One records, Vettel has failed to win his first four German Grand Prix races.

AUSTRALIAN GRAND PRIX
ALBERT PARK, MELBOURNE

FIRST RACE: 1996
CIRCUIT LENGTH: 5.303 KM
LAPS: 58
BUILT: 1996
CAPACITY: 80,000
RECORD CROWD: 300,000
(OVER 4 DAYS)

MALAYSIAN GRAND PRIX
SEPANG INTERNATIONAL CIRCUIT, KUALA LUMPUR

FIRST RACE: 1999
CIRCUIT LENGTH: 5.543 KM
LAPS: 56
BUILT: 1998
CAPACITY: 130,000
RECORD CROWD: 115,794

CHINESE GRAND PRIX
SHANGHAI CIRCUIT, SHANGAI

FIRST RACE: 2004
CIRCUIT LENGTH: 5.451 KM
LAPS: 56
BUILT: 2003/2004
CAPACITY: 200,000

03

TURKISH GRAND PRIX
ISTANBUL PARK CIRCUIT, ISTANBUL

FIRST RACE: 2005
CIRCUIT LENGTH: 5.338 KM
LAPS: 58
BUILT: 2005
CAPACITY: 155,000
RECORD CROWD: 40,000

04

DRIVERPROFILES

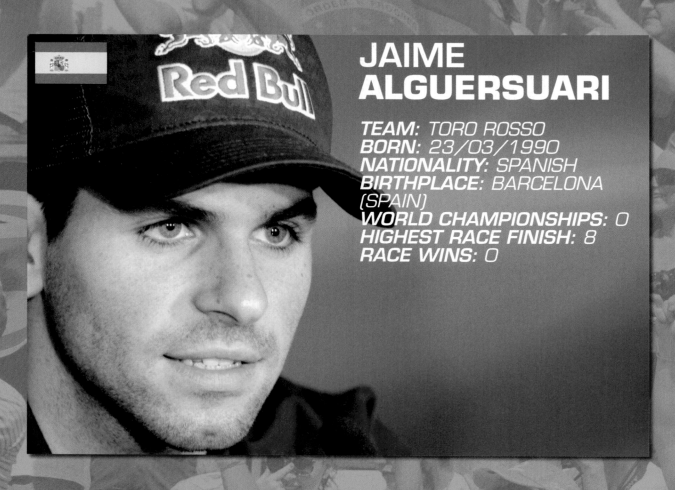

JAIME ALGUERSUARI

TEAM: TORO ROSSO
BORN: 23/03/1990
NATIONALITY: SPANISH
BIRTHPLACE: BARCELONA (SPAIN)
WORLD CHAMPIONSHIPS: 0
HIGHEST RACE FINISH: 8
RACE WINS: 0

FERNANDO ALONSO

TEAM: FERRARI
BORN: 29/07/1981
NATIONALITY: SPANISH
BIRTHPLACE: OVIEDO (SPAIN)
WORLD CHAMPIONSHIPS: 2
HIGHEST RACE FINISH: 1
RACE WINS: 27

JEROME D'AMBROSIO

TEAM: *VIRGIN*
BORN: *27/12/1985*
NATIONALITY: *BELGIAN*
BIRTHPLACE: *ETTERBEEK (BELGIUM)*
WORLD CHAMPIONSHIPS: *0*
HIGHEST RACE FINISH: *14*
RACE WINS: *0*

RUBENS BARRICHELLO

TEAM: *WILLIAMS*
BORN: *23/05/1972*
NATIONALITY: *BRAZILIAN*
BIRTHPLACE: *SAO PAULO (BRAZIL)*
WORLD CHAMPIONSHIPS: *0*
HIGHEST RACE FINISH: *1*
RACE WINS: *11*

SPANISH GRAND PRIX
CIRCUIT DE CATALUNYA, BARCELONA

FIRST RACE: 1991
CIRCUIT LENGTH: 4.655 KM
LAPS: 66
BUILT: 1991
CAPACITY: 67,730

MONACO
CIRCUIT DE MONACO, MONTE CARLO

FIRST RACE: 1950
CIRCUIT LENGTH: 3.340 KM
LAPS: 78
BUILT: 1950 (STREET CIRCUIT)
CAPACITY: 50,000

CANADIAN GRAND PRIX
CIRCUIT GILLES VILLENEUVE, MONTREAL

CIRCUIT LENGTH: 4.361 KM
LAPS: 70
BUILT: 1978
CAPACITY: 100,000
RECORD CROWD: 100,000

EUROPEAN GRAND PRIX (SPAIN)
STREET CIRCUIT, VALENCIA

FIRST RACE: 2008
CIRCUIT LENGTH: 5.419 KM
LAPS: 57
BUILT: 2008 (STREET CIRCUIT)
CAPACITY: 112,771

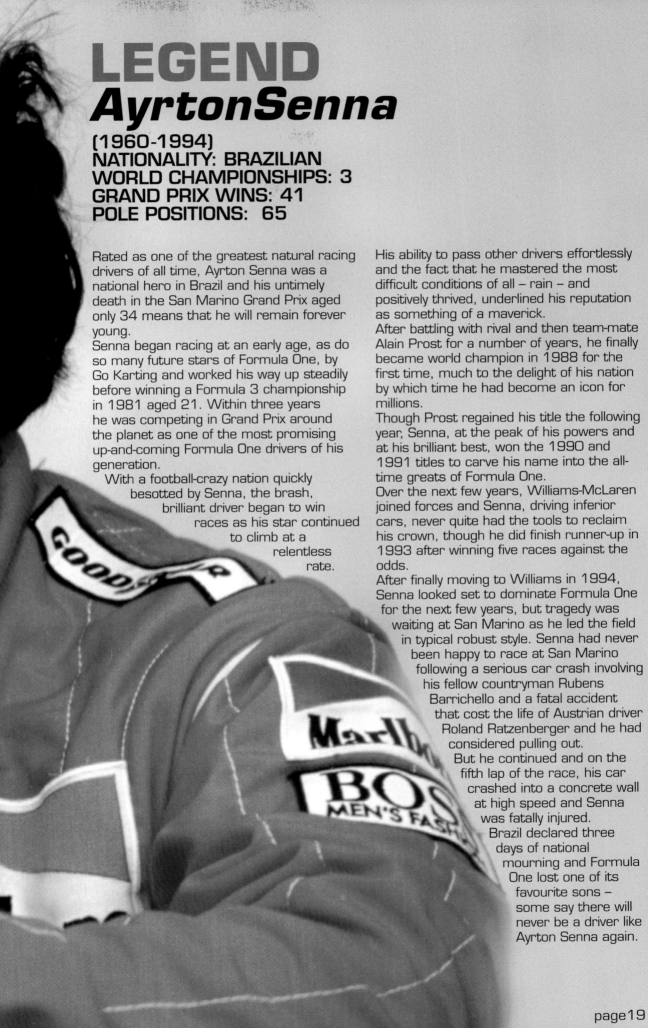

LEGEND
AyrtonSenna

(1960-1994)
NATIONALITY: BRAZILIAN
WORLD CHAMPIONSHIPS: 3
GRAND PRIX WINS: 41
POLE POSITIONS: 65

Rated as one of the greatest natural racing drivers of all time, Ayrton Senna was a national hero in Brazil and his untimely death in the San Marino Grand Prix aged only 34 means that he will remain forever young.

Senna began racing at an early age, as do so many future stars of Formula One, by Go Karting and worked his way up steadily before winning a Formula 3 championship in 1981 aged 21. Within three years he was competing in Grand Prix around the planet as one of the most promising up-and-coming Formula One drivers of his generation.

With a football-crazy nation quickly besotted by Senna, the brash, brilliant driver began to win races as his star continued to climb at a relentless rate.

His ability to pass other drivers effortlessly and the fact that he mastered the most difficult conditions of all – rain – and positively thrived, underlined his reputation as something of a maverick.

After battling with rival and then team-mate Alain Prost for a number of years, he finally became world champion in 1988 for the first time, much to the delight of his nation by which time he had become an icon for millions.

Though Prost regained his title the following year, Senna, at the peak of his powers and at his brilliant best, won the 1990 and 1991 titles to carve his name into the all-time greats of Formula One.

Over the next few years, Williams-McLaren joined forces and Senna, driving inferior cars, never quite had the tools to reclaim his crown, though he did finish runner-up in 1993 after winning five races against the odds.

After finally moving to Williams in 1994, Senna looked set to dominate Formula One for the next few years, but tragedy was waiting at San Marino as he led the field in typical robust style. Senna had never been happy to race at San Marino following a serious car crash involving his fellow countryman Rubens Barrichello and a fatal accident that cost the life of Austrian driver Roland Ratzenberger and he had considered pulling out.

But he continued and on the fifth lap of the race, his car crashed into a concrete wall at high speed and Senna was fatally injured.

Brazil declared three days of national mourning and Formula One lost one of its favourite sons – some say there will never be a driver like Ayrton Senna again.

Lewis Hamilton

SPOT THE DIFFERENCE

PICTURE A AND B ARE THE SAME – OR ARE THEY? CAN YOU SPOT AND CIRCLE THE SIX DIFFERENCES IN PICTURE B?

Answers on page 58

DRIVERPROFILES

SÉBASTIEN BUEMI

TEAM: *TORO ROSSO*
BORN: *31/10/1988*
NATIONALITY: *SWISS*
BIRTHPLACE: *AIGLE (SWITZERLAND)*
WORLD CHAMPIONSHIPS: *0*
HIGHEST RACE FINISH: *7*
RACE WINS: *0*

JENSON BUTTON

TEAM: *MCLAREN*
BORN: *19/01/1980*
NATIONALITY: *BRITISH*
BIRTHPLACE: *FROME (ENGLAND)*
WORLD CHAMPIONSHIPS: *1*
HIGHEST RACE FINISH: *1*
RACE WINS: *11*

TIMO
GLOCK

TEAM: *VIRGIN*
BORN: *18/03/1982*
NATIONALITY: *GERMAN*
BIRTHPLACE: *LINDENFELS (GERMANY)*
WORLD CHAMPIONSHIPS: *0*
HIGHEST RACE FINISH: *2*
RACE WINS: *0*

LEWIS
HAMILTON

TEAM: *MCLAREN*
BORN: *07/01/1985*
NATIONALITY: *BRITISH*
BIRTHPLACE: *STEVENAGE (ENGLAND)*
WORLD CHAMPIONSHIPS: *1*
HIGHEST RACE FINISH: *1*
RACE WINS: *16*

*DETAILS CORRECT TO 5TH AUGUST 2011

Paul di Resta

GUESS WHO?

HERE ARE FOUR IMAGES OF SOME CURRENT F1 STARS, CAN YOU GUESS WHO THEY ARE?

Answers on page 59

BRITISH GRAND PRIX
SILVERSTONE CIRCUIT, NORTHANTS

FIRST RACE: 1950
CIRCUIT LENGTH: 5.891 KM
LAPS: 52
BUILT: 1948
CAPACITY: 90,000
RECORD CROWD: 310,000 (OVER THREE DAYS) IN 2009

09

F1WORDSEARCH CIRCUITS

CAN YOU FIND THE 10 FORMULA ONE CIRCUITS IN THE GRID BELOW? REMEMBER, THE WORDS CAN BE UP, DOWN, DIAGONAL OR HORIZONTAL.

YAS MARINA, MONZA, MONACO, SILVERSTONE, SEPANG, NURBURGRING, MARINA BAY, INTERLAGOS, VALENCIA, NEW DELHI

```
Z Y A B A N I R A M N N R
L A N N Q H K N P J U A K
S N T W J H H R L R M I Y
R I V S X N K F B W H C W
H R L H O G X U V I K N G
V A S V T G R L H L A E Z
K M E R E G A L Z Z D L R
X S P K R R E L N N D A R
F A A I Q D S O R P P V K
C Y N R W T M T L E N M N
N G G E R X Q N O M T M B
X Q N N T J M K L N G N L
M O N A C O Y T H J E W I
```

F1 CROSSWORD

READ THE CLUES AND PUT THE ANSWERS INTO THE CROSSWORD
PUZZLE. SEE IF YOU CAN FILL EVERY BLANK IN THE BOX!

ACROSS

02 A vital part of a driver's safety equipment (6)
07 The fastest car in qualifying gets to start here (4, 8)
10 A place drivers love to climb (6)
11 This is where drivers head for a brief pause in the race (3, 4)
14 Monaco's racing track is set here (5, 5)
16 Adrian Sutil drives for this team (5, 5)
18 These guys watch the race very closely and make judgements if necessary (8)
19 This is the vehicle that makes sure the track is OK before the race begins and after an incident (6, 3)
20 The device that determines which direction the Formula One cars go in (8, 5)

DOWN

01 This coloured flag indicates danger during a race (6)
03 A tight sequence of corners is known as a _____ (7)
04 Britain's home Formula One circuit (11)
05 What every driver hopes to see (9, 4)
06 These electronic blankets are sometimes wrapped around certain parts of the car before being fitted (4, 7)
08 You need to do this to get past the person in front! (8)
09 These tyres are crucial if it rains (3, 7)
12 Lewis and Jenson drive for this team (7)
13 The 2010 winners of the Constructors' Championship (3, 4)
15 The amount of points the winner gets for winning a Formula One race (3)
17 Fixed weights around the car to achieve balance (7)

Answers on page 59

Michael Schumacher

Mercedes-Benz

DRIVERPROFILES

NICK HEIDFELD

TEAM: *RENAULT*
BORN: *10/05/1977*
NATIONALITY: *GERMAN*
BIRTHPLACE: *MONCHENGLADBACH (GERMANY)*
WORLD CHAMPIONSHIPS: *0*
HIGHEST RACE FINISH: *2*
RACE WINS: *0*

NARAIN KARTHIKEYAN

TEAM: *HRT*
BORN: *14/01/1977*
NATIONALITY: *INDIAN*
BIRTHPLACE: *CHENNAI (INDIA)*
WORLD CHAMPIONSHIPS: *0*
HIGHEST RACE FINISH: *4*
RACE WINS: *0*

KARTHIKEYAN WAS TEMPORARILY REPLACED BY DANIEL RICCIARDO FOR THE SECOND HALF OF THE 2011 SEASON

KAMUI
KOBAYASHI

TEAM: *SAUBER*
BORN: *13/09/1986*
NATIONALITY: *JAPANESE*
BIRTHPLACE: *HYOGO (JAPAN)*
WORLD CHAMPIONSHIPS: *0*
HIGHEST RACE FINISH: *5*
RACE WINS: *0*

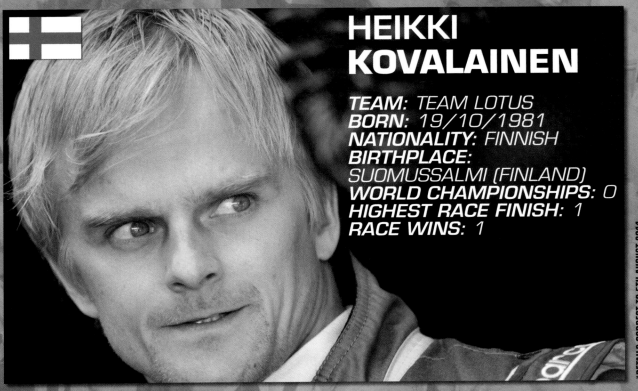

HEIKKI
KOVALAINEN

TEAM: *TEAM LOTUS*
BORN: *19/10/1981*
NATIONALITY: *FINNISH*
BIRTHPLACE:
SUOMUSSALMI (FINLAND)
WORLD CHAMPIONSHIPS: *0*
HIGHEST RACE FINISH: *1*
RACE WINS: *1*

*DETAILS CORRECT TO 5TH AUGUST 2011

GERMAN GRAND PRIX
NÜRBURGRING CIRCUIT, NURBURG

FIRST RACE: 1984
CIRCUIT LENGTH: 5.148 KM
LAPS: 60
BUILT: 1984
CAPACITY: 400,000
RECORD CROWD: 310,000

HUNGARIAN GRAND PRIX
HUNGARORING CIRCUIT, BUDAPEST

FIRST RACE: 1986
CIRCUIT LENGTH: 4.381 KM
LAPS: 70
BUILT: 1986
CAPACITY: 120,000
RECORD CROWD: 200,000
(OVER THREE DAYS) IN 2008

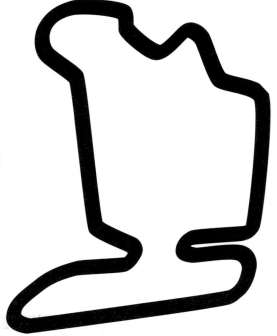

BELGIAN GRAND PRIX
SPA FRANCORCHAMPS CIRCUIT, FRANCORCHAMPS

FIRST RACE: 1983 (REVISED SHORTER VERSION)
CIRCUIT LENGTH: 7.004 KM
LAPS: 44
BUILT: 1924 (STREET CIRCUIT)
CAPACITY: AROUND 90,000
RECORD CROWD: 150,000 (OVER THREE DAYS)

ITALIAN GRAND PRIX
MONZA CIRCUIT, MONZA

FIRST RACE: 1950
CIRCUIT LENGTH: 5.793 KM
LAPS: 53
BUILT: 1950
CAPACITY: 115,000
RECORD CROWD: 100,000

F1 WORDSEARCH DRIVERS

CAN YOU FIND THE 10 FORMULA ONE DRIVER SURNAMES IN THE GRID BELOW? REMEMBER, THE WORDS CAN BE UP, DOWN, DIAGONAL OR HORIZONTAL.

HAMILTON, BUTTON, ALONSO, VETTEL, MASSA, WEBBER, SCHUMACHER, ROSBERG, HEIDFELD, PETROV

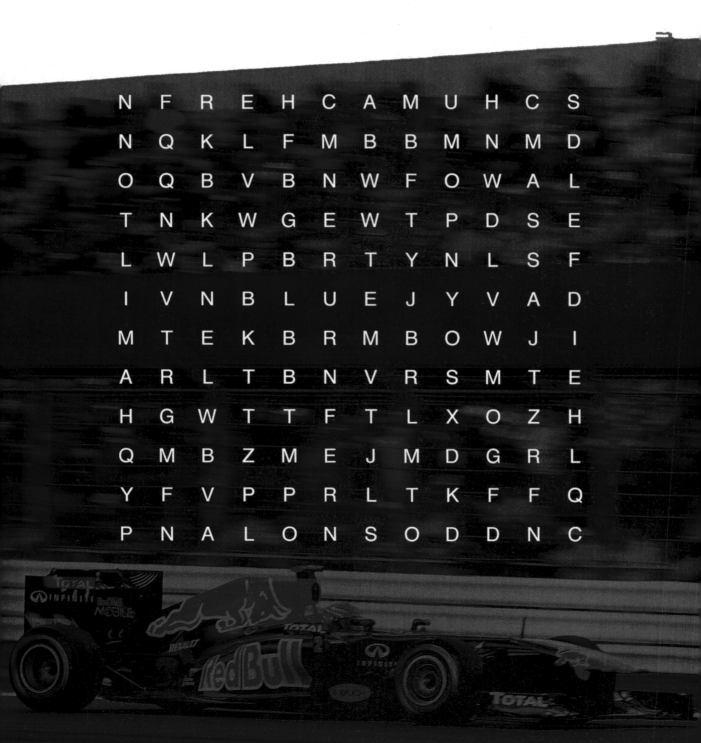

```
N F R E H C A M U H C S
N Q K L F M B B M N M D
O Q B V B N W F O W A L
T N K W G E W T P D S E
L W L P B R T Y N L S F
I V N B L U E J Y V A D
M T E K B R M B O W J I
A R L T B N V R S M T E
H G W T T F T L X O Z H
Q M B Z M E J M D G R L
Y F V P P R L T K F F Q
P N A L O N S O D D N C
```

Jenson
Button

THE BIG F1 QUIZ 2012

CAN YOU CLIMB THE PODIUM? CAN YOU EARN ENOUGH POINTS TO WIN THE CHALLENGE? SEE HOW YOU GO – THE POINTS ARE IN BRACKETS AND WHEN YOU'VE TOTTED UP YOUR SCORE, CHECK WHERE YOU'VE FINISHED!

1 WHICH TYRE SUPPLIER HAD ITS LAST YEAR OF BEING SOLE SUPPLIER TO F1 IN 2010?
A) BRIDGESTONE B) PIRELLI C) DUNLOP (4 POINTS)

2 WHICH FOUR DRIVERS WENT INTO THE FINAL GRAND PRIX OF THE SEASON WITH A CHANCE OF BECOMING WORLD CHAMPION IN 2010? (1 POINT FOR EACH)

6 NAME TWO TEAMS WHO HAD TO PULL OUT OF THE 2010 CHAMPIONSHIP. (2 POINTS EACH)

7 WHICH TEAM DID FERNANDO ALONSO LEAVE RENAULT FOR? (1 POINT)

8 WHO BOUGHT OUT JENSON BUTTON'S FORMER TEAM BRAWN GP? (2 POINTS)

3 AT WHICH TRACK DID A ONE-TWO FINISH GUARANTEE RED BULL RACING THEIR FIRST EVER CONSTRUCTORS' CHAMPIONSHIP?
A) ABU DHABI B) BRAZIL C) MALAYSIA (2 POINTS)

4 MICHAEL SCHUMACHER RETURNED TO F1 AFTER HE CAME OUT OF RETIREMENT – HOW MANY YEARS HAD HE BEEN ABSENT FOR? A) ONE B) TWO C) THREE (2 POINTS)

5 WHAT DO THE INITIALS IN THE F1'S GOVERNING BODY – THE FIA – STAND FOR? (4 POINTS)

9 WHAT IS AYRTON SENNA'S NEPHEW CALLED AND WHICH TEAM DOES HE DRIVE FOR? (2 POINTS EACH)

10 VITALY PETROV IS RUSSIA'S FIRST EVER F1 DRIVER. TRUE OR FALSE? (1 POINT)

11 WHICH FINNISH DRIVER TOOK A YEAR OUT FROM F1? (1 POINT)

12 WHAT IS NICO ROSBERG'S FATHER CALLED? A) KEKE B) NANDO C) RICO (1 POINT)

13 WHO DOES KAMUI KOBAYASHI DRIVE FOR? (1 POINT)

14 WHICH CIRCUIT HAS THE MOST LAPS OF ALL THE F1 TRACKS?
A) ABU DHABI B) AUSTRALIA
C) MONACO (2 POINTS)

15 WITH THE FIRST GRAND PRIX HELD IN 1922, WHAT IS THE OLDEST CIRCUIT STILL BEING USED BY THE F1 TODAY? A) SILVERSTONE B) YAS MARINA C) MONZA (2 POINTS)

16 WHO IS STEFANO DOMENICALI THE BOSS OF? A) LOTUS B) FORCE INDIA C) FERRARI (5 POINTS)

17 BRITISH TEAM MCLAREN ARE BASED WHERE IN ENGLAND?
A) MANCHESTER B) OXFORD
C) WOKING (5 POINTS)

18 HOW MANY POINTS DID SEBASTIAN VETTEL WIN THE 2010 WORLD CHAMPIONSHIP BY?
A) 10PTS B) 6PTS C) 4PTS (1 POINT)

19 NAME THE POLISH F1 DRIVER SERIOUSLY INJURED IN THE 2011 RONDE DI ANDORA RALLY. (3 POINTS)

20 WHICH CURRENT F1 DRIVER WAS BORN IN SAO PAULO? (1 POINT)

HOW DID YOU DO?

46-50PTS – RACE WINNER – 5 LAPS AHEAD OF EVERYONE ELSE!

40-45PTS – YOU'RE ON THE PODIUM AS A RUNNER UP – WELL DONE!

35-39PTS – THIRD PLACE – GREAT EFFORT!

25-34PTS – YOU'VE FINISHED THE RACE AND PICKED UP SOME CHAMPIONSHIP POINTS.

15-24PTS – DRIVE THROUGH PENALTY SEES YOU STRUGGLE TO GET OVER THE FINISH LINE – TOO MANY PIT STOPS!

14PTS OR LESS – YOU USED THE WRONG TYRES AND SKIDDED OFF – BETTER LUCK NEXT TIME!

Answers on page 58

HEAD 2HEAD

LewisHamilton JensonButton

THEY ARE THE BEST BRITISH DRIVERS IN FORMULA ONE – BUT WHICH IS THE GREATER TALENT: LEWIS OR JENSON? WE TRY TO GET TO THE BOTTOM OF THE PUZZLE IN OUR SPECIAL HEAD2HEAD TEST…

PODIUMS:
Jenson 36
Lewis 40

WORLD CHAMPIONSHIPS:
Jenson 1
Lewis 1

RACE WINS:
Jenson 11
Lewis 16

POLE POSITIONS:
Jenson 7
Lewis 18

CHAMPIONSHIP POINTS:
Jenson 675
Lewis 642

FASTEST LAPS:
Jenson 3
Lewis 9

GRAND PRIX ENTERED:
Jenson 202
Lewis 82

BRITISH GRAND PRIX POINTS:
Jenson 27
Lewis 46

CONCLUSION:

On hard data, Lewis Hamilton is the better driver. He's only been around since 2007 while Jenson Button began in 2000, but Lewis has arguably driven better cars in his short career. While Lewis was groomed to be a champion from an early age, Jenson's path has been more difficult and he has had to rely more on raw talent at certain times. When Jenson was finally given a car that matched his ability, he won the Formula One championship at the first time of asking. In short, both drivers are very different, but very talented and the pride of British F1 racing – Lewis edges most of the categories, though when it comes to adverse weather conditions, few are better than Jenson so it's a desperately close thing.

*ALL DATA CORRECT TO 5TH AUGUST 2011

DRIVERPROFILES

VITANTONIO LIUZZI

TEAM: HRT
BORN: 08/06/1981
NATIONALITY: ITALIAN
BIRTHPLACE: LOCOROTONDO (ITALY)
WORLD CHAMPIONSHIPS: 0
HIGHEST RACE FINISH: 6
RACE WINS: 0

PASTOR MALDONADO

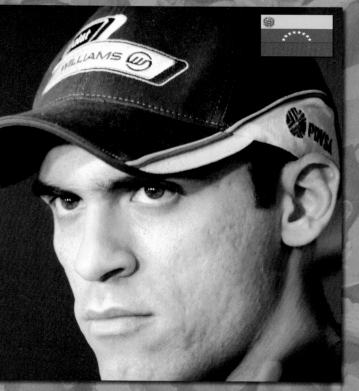

TEAM: WILLIAMS
BORN: 09/03/1985
NATIONALITY: VENEZUELAN
BIRTHPLACE: MARACAY (VENEZUELA)
WORLD CHAMPIONSHIPS: 0
HIGHEST RACE FINISH: 14
RACE WINS: 0

FELIPE MASSA

TEAM: FERRARI
BORN: 25/04/1981
NATIONALITY: BRAZILIAN
BIRTHPLACE: SAO PAULO (BRAZIL)
WORLD CHAMPIONSHIPS: 0
HIGHEST RACE FINISH: 1
RACE WINS: 11

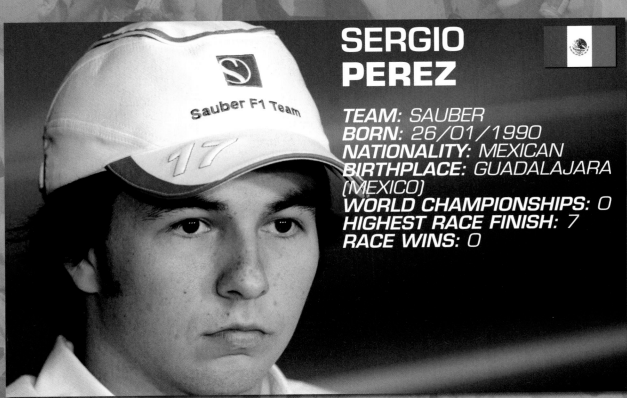

SERGIO PEREZ

TEAM: SAUBER
BORN: 26/01/1990
NATIONALITY: MEXICAN
BIRTHPLACE: GUADALAJARA (MEXICO)
WORLD CHAMPIONSHIPS: 0
HIGHEST RACE FINISH: 7
RACE WINS: 0

*DETAILS CORRECT TO 5TH AUGUST 2011

SPOT THE DIFFERENCE

PICTURE A AND B ARE THE SAME – OR ARE THEY? CAN YOU SPOT AND CIRCLE THE SIX DIFFERENCES IN PICTURE B?

Answers on page 58

WHICHCIRCUIT?

CAN YOU WORK OUT WHICH CIRCUIT THE IMAGES HERE WERE TAKEN AT?

Answers on page 59

THE 2011 SAFETY CAR:
All you need to know!

EVER WONDERED WHAT THE SAFETY CAR IS OR WHY IT'S SOMETIMES USED AND WHO DRIVES IT? WELL, HERE ARE THE ANSWERS TO ALL THE ABOVE QUESTIONS – AND MORE!

- The 2011 Safety Car is a Mercedes-Benz SLS AMG luxury grand tourer automobile developed by Mercedes-AMG to replace the Mercedes-Benz SLR McLaren of 2010.

- Its market value is 177,000 Euros (around £135,000).

- It has a 6.3 litre V8 engine, seven speed double-clutch transmission and composite brakes.

- The light bar on the Safety Car's roof has two orange flashing lights and two cameras – the car also has two monitors in the cockpit to keep track of the race and other developments.

- The 2011 Safety Car driver is Bernd Maylander - a role he has held since 2000.

- The Safety Car first appeared in 1973, though it wasn't until 1992 that the FIA laid down clear guidelines.

- The FIA race director makes the decision when the Safety Car is to be deployed on the race track.

- Drivers are informed in three ways that the Safety Car is on the track – a light in their cockpit, a yellow flag and via a radio message.

- Each lap the Safety Car completes counts as a completed race lap – if the hazard that caused its appearance isn't solved or driving conditions don't improve, the race can finish with the Safety Car crossing the line and the cars behind finishing in the positions they have remained in since the Safety Car appeared.

- Historically, the three circuits least likely to see the Safety Car deployed in are Malaysia, Hungary and Bahrain – all of which have excellent safety records and substantial run-off areas for cars.

- The record laps for a Safety Car came in Japan in 2007 when 26 laps were completed.

- The two main reasons for Safety Car deployment is a waterlogged track or an accident.

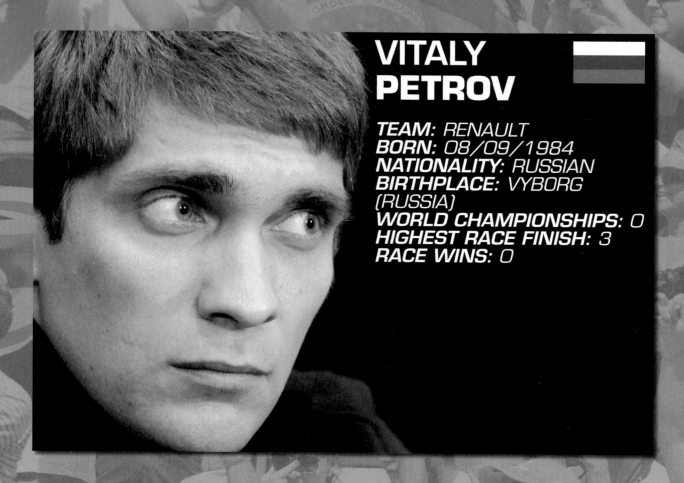

VITALY PETROV

TEAM: *RENAULT*
BORN: *08/09/1984*
NATIONALITY: *RUSSIAN*
BIRTHPLACE: *VYBORG (RUSSIA)*
WORLD CHAMPIONSHIPS: *0*
HIGHEST RACE FINISH: *3*
RACE WINS: *0*

PAUL DI RESTA

TEAM: *FORCE INDIA*
BORN: *16/04/1986*
NATIONALITY: *BRITISH*
BIRTHPLACE: *UPHALL (SCOTLAND)*
WORLD CHAMPIONSHIPS: *0*
HIGHEST RACE FINISH: *7*
RACE WINS: *0*

NICO ROSBERG

TEAM: MERCEDES
BORN: 27/06/1985
NATIONALITY: GERMAN
BIRTHPLACE: WIESBADEN (GERMANY)
WORLD CHAMPIONSHIPS: 0
HIGHEST RACE FINISH: 2
RACE WINS: 0

MICHAEL SCHUMACHER

TEAM: MERCEDES
BORN: 03/01/1969
NATIONALITY: GERMAN
BIRTHPLACE: HURTH-HERMULHEIM (GERMANY)
WORLD CHAMPIONSHIPS: 7
HIGHEST RACE FINISH: 1
RACE WINS: 91

*DETAILS CORRECT TO 5TH AUGUST 2011

SINGAPORE GRAND PRIX
MARINA BAY SINGAPORE

FIRST RACE: 2008
CIRCUIT LENGTH: 5.073 KM
LAPS: 61
BUILT: 2008 (STREET CIRCUIT)
CAPACITY: 100,000
RECORD CROWD: 100,000 IN 2008

14

JAPANESE GRAND PRIX
SUZUKA INTERNATIONAL RACING CIRCUIT

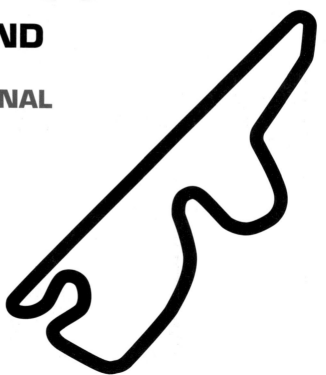

FIRST RACE: 1962
CIRCUIT LENGTH: 5.807 KM
LAPS: 53
BUILT: 1962
CAPACITY: 100,000
RECORD CROWD: 100,000

15

SOUTH KOREAN GRAND PRIX
KOREA INTERNATIONAL CIRCUIT

FIRST RACE: 2010
CIRCUIT LENGTH: 5.615 KM
LAPS: 55
BUILT: 2010
CAPACITY: 135,000

INDIAN GRAND PRIX
BUDDH INTERNATIONAL CIRCUIT

FIRST RACE: 2011
CIRCUIT LENGTH: 5.137 KM
LAPS: 60
BUILT: 2011
CAPACITY: 110,000

Fernando Alonso

HELMET QUIZ

CAN YOU MATCH THESE HELMETS BELOW WITH THE F1 DRIVERS THEY BELONG TO?

Answers on page 58

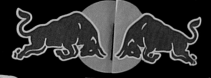

ABU DHABI GRAND PRIX
YAS MARINA CIRCUIT – YAS ISLAND, ABU DHABI

FIRST RACE: 2009
CIRCUIT LENGTH: 5.554 KM
LAPS: 55
BUILT: 2009
CAPACITY: 41,093

BRAZILIAN GRAND PRIX
AUTODROMO JOSE CARLOS PACE, SAO PAULO

FIRST RACE: 1973
CIRCUIT LENGTH: 4.309 KM
LAPS: 71
BUILT: 1940
CAPACITY: 80,000

ONE TO WATCH:
PAUL DI RESTA

HE'S BEATEN SEBASTIAN VETTEL AND LEWIS HAMILTON AT JUNIOR LEVEL SO NOBODY SHOULD BE SURPRISED THAT PAUL DI RESTA IS FINALLY MAKING A NAME FOR HIMSELF...

One of Formula One's rising stars is Britain's Paul di Resta, who joined Force India as one of the 2011 season's new drivers. At 25, he's probably past the rookie status, but he has shown enough talent to suggest he can carve a fine career out for himself over the next few years.

Di Resta is from Uphall in West Lothian and he hopes to follow in the footsteps of another great Scottish Formula One driver – his hero, David Coulthard. Racing is in Di Resta's blood, being the cousin of racing drivers Dario and Marino Franchitti. Continuing the sporting links, his late step-father was Scottish footballer Dougie McCracken.

Like many future Formula One drivers, Di Resta started his career in Karting, winning the British JICA Championship in 2001 aged 15. He gradually worked his way through the ranks and won the ASM Formula 3 championship ahead of future Formula One World Drivers Champion Sebastian Vettel. He continued to race in various disciplines and cars across Europe with varying degrees of success and always with one eye cast on the glamour of Formula One. Sponsorship problems undoubtedly held the young Scot's career up, but he wasn't about to let go of his dream of becoming a Grand Prix driver.

After clinching the 2010 DTM Championship, Di Resta, who had tested for the Force India and McLaren teams in 2009, finally clinched a dream deal with Force India to race in the 2010 Formula One season as reserve driver and took part in the 2010 Australian Grand Prix during the first free practice session.

A year later he became one of Force India's first choice driving team alongside Adrian Sutil, replacing Vitantonio Liuzzi, making his Formula One debut in Bahrain and claiming his first championship point at the 2011 Australian Grand Prix. Watch out for him on the racetrack!

FACT FILE:

Name: Paul di Resta
Height: 185 cm
Weight: 78 kg
Team: Force India
Debut: Bahrain GP 2011
Date of birth: 16 April 1986

Birthplace: Uphall, Scotland
Race wins: 0
Poles : 0
Podiums: 0
F1 career points: 8
Championships: 0

* DETAILS CORRECT TO 5TH AUGUST 2011

DRIVERPROFILES

ADRIAN SUTIL

TEAM: *FORCE INDIA*
BORN: *11/01/1983*
NATIONALITY: *GERMAN*
BIRTHPLACE: *STARNBERG (GERMANY)*
WORLD CHAMPIONSHIPS: *0*
HIGHEST RACE FINISH: *4*
RACE WINS: *0*

JARNO TRULLI

TEAM: *TEAM LOTUS*
BORN: *13/07/1974*
NATIONALITY: *ITALIAN*
BIRTHPLACE: *PESCARA (ITALY)*
WORLD CHAMPIONSHIPS: *0*
HIGHEST RACE FINISH: *1*
RACE WINS: *1*

SEBASTIAN VETTEL

TEAM: *RED BULL RACING*
BORN: *03/07/1987*
NATIONALITY: *GERMAN*
BIRTHPLACE: *HEPPENHEIM (GERMANY)*
WORLD CHAMPIONSHIPS: *1*
HIGHEST RACE FINISH: *1*
RACE WINS: *16*

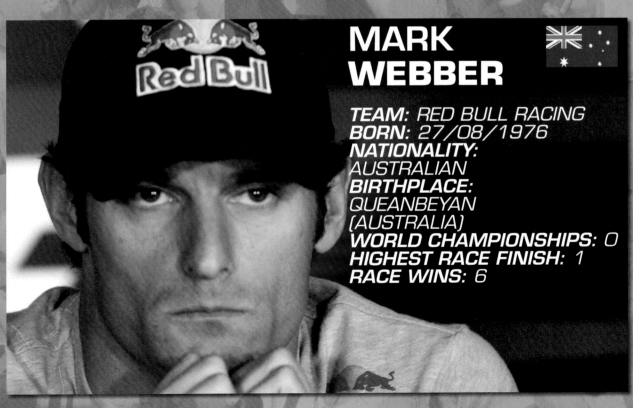

MARK WEBBER

TEAM: *RED BULL RACING*
BORN: *27/08/1976*
NATIONALITY: *AUSTRALIAN*
BIRTHPLACE: *QUEANBEYAN (AUSTRALIA)*
WORLD CHAMPIONSHIPS: *0*
HIGHEST RACE FINISH: *1*
RACE WINS: *6*

QUIZANSWERS

THEBIG F1QUIZ

ANSWERS FROM (PG 36-37)

1, A) BRIDGESTONE
2, SEBASTIAN VETTEL, MARK WEBBER, FERNANDO ALONSO, LEWIS HAMILTON
3, B) BRAZIL
4, C) THREE
5, FÉDÉRATION INTERNATIONALE DE L'AUTOMOBILE
6, TOYOTA AND BMW
7, FERRARI
8, MERCEDES GP
9, BRUNO, HISPANIA
10, TRUE
11, KIMI RAIKONNEN
12, A) KEKE
13, SAUBER-FERRARI
14, C) MONACO – 78 LAPS
15, C) MONZA
16, C) FERRARI
17, C) WOKING
18, C) 4 POINTS
19, ROBERT KUBICA
20, FELIPE MASSA

SPOT THE DIFFERENCE ANSWERS (PG 21)

HELMET QUIZ ANSWERS (PG 51)

KAMUI KOBAYASHI

LEWIS HAMILTON

JENSON BUTTON

SPOT THE DIFFERENCE ANSWERS (PG 42)

NICK HEIDFELD

WORDSEARCH SOLUTION (PG 27)

CROSSWORD SOLUTION (PG 28)

Solution:

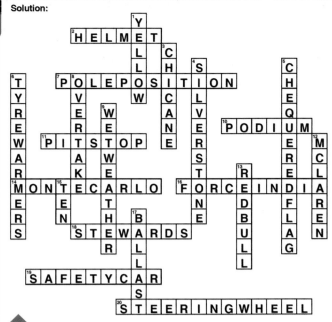

WORDSEARCH SOLUTION (PG 34)

GUESS WHO?
ANSWERS (PG 25)

1, Fernando Alonso

2, Jenson Button

3, Sebastian Vettel

4, Lewis Hamilton

WHICH CIRCUIT?
ANSWERS
(PG 43)

A) MONACO
B) MALAYSIA
C) CHINA
D) ABU DHABI

FORMULA ONE ROLL OF HONOUR

HERE IS A LIST OF THE CHAMPION DRIVERS WHO, OVER THE COURSE OF THE F1 SEASON, PROVED THEY WERE THE BEST...

YEAR	CHAMPIONS	CONSTRUCTORS
2010	Sebastian VETTEL (GER)	Red Bull
2009	Jenson BUTTON (GBR)	Brawn-Mercedes
2008	Lewis HAMILTON (GBR)	Ferrari
2007	Kimi RAIKKONEN (FIN)	Ferrari
2006	Fernando ALONSO (SPA)	Renault
2005	Fernando ALONSO (SPA)	Renault
2004	Michael SCHUMACHER (GER)	Ferrari
2003	Michael SCHUMACHER (GER)	Ferrari
2002	Michael SCHUMACHER (GER)	Ferrari
2001	Michael SCHUMACHER (GER)	Ferrari
2000	Michael SCHUMACHER (GER)	Ferrari
1999	Mika HAKKINEN (FIN)	Ferrari
1998	Mika HAKKINEN (FIN)	McLaren - Mercedes
1997	Jacques VILLENEUVE (CAN)	Williams - Renault
1996	Damon HILL (GBR)	Williams - Renault
1995	Michael SCHUMACHER (GER)	Benetton - Renault
1994	Michael SCHUMACHER (GER)	Williams - Renault
1993	Alain PROST (FRA)	Williams - Renault
1992	Nigel MANSELL (GBR)	Williams - Renault
1991	Ayrton SENNA (BRA)	McLaren - Honda
1990	Ayrton SENNA (BRA)	McLaren - Honda
1989	Alain PROST (FRA)	McLaren - Honda
1988	Ayrton SENNA (BRA)	McLaren - Honda
1987	Nelson PIQUET (BRA)	Williams - Honda
1986	Alain PROST (FRA)	Williams - Honda
1985	Alain PROST (FRA)	McLaren - TAG/Porsche
1984	Niki LAUDA (AUT)	McLaren - TAG/Porsche
1983	Nelson PIQUET (BRA)	Ferrari
1982	Keke ROSBERG (FIN)	Ferrari
1981	Nelson PIQUET (BRA)	Williams - Ford/Cosworth
1980	Alan JONES (AUS)	Williams - Ford/Cosworth

1979	Jody SCHECKTER (SAF)	Ferrari
1978	Mario ANDRETTI (USA)	Lotus - Ford/Cosworth
1977	Niki LAUDA (AUT)	Ferrari
1976	James HUNT (GBR)	Ferrari
1975	Niki LAUDA (AUT)	Ferrari
1974	Emerson FITTIPALDI (BRA)	McLaren - Ford/Cosworth
1973	Jackie STEWART (GBR)	Lotus - Ford/Cosworth
1972	Emerson FITTIPALDI (BRA)	Lotus - Ford/Cosworth
1971	Jackie STEWART (GBR)	Tyrrell - Ford/Cosworth
1970	Jochen RINDT (AUT)	Lotus - Ford/Cosworth
1969	Jackie STEWART (GBR)	Matra - Ford/Cosworth
1968	Graham HILL (GBR)	Lotus - Ford/Cosworth
1967	Denny HULME (NZL)	Brabham - Repco
1966	Jack BRABHAM (AUS)	Brabham - Repco
1965	Jim CLARK (GBR)	Lotus - Climax
1964	John SURTEES (GBR)	Ferrari
1963	Jim CLARK (GBR)	Lotus - Climax
1962	Graham HILL (GBR)	BRM
1961	Phil HILL (USA)	Ferrari
1960	Jack BRABHAM (AUS)	Cooper - Climax
1959	Jack BRABHAM (AUS)	Cooper - Climax
1958	Mike HAWTHORN (GBR)	Vanwall
1957	Juan Manuel FANGIO (ARG)	Independent
1956	Juan Manuel FANGIO (ARG)	Independent
1955	Juan Manuel FANGIO (ARG)	Independent
1954	Juan Manuel FANGIO (ARG)	Independent
1953	Alberto ASCARI (ITA)	Independent
1952	Alberto ASCARI (ITA)	Independent
1951	Juan Manuel FANGIO (ARG)	Independent
1950	Giuseppe 'Nino' FARINA (ITA)	Independent